That Costs Two Shells

The History of Money

by Nancy Loewen * illustrated by Brian Jensen

Thanks to our advisers for their expertise, research, and advice:

Dr. Joseph Santos
Associate Professor of Economics, Department of Economics
South Dakota State University

Susan Kesselring, M.A., Literacy Educator
Rosemount–Apple Valley–Eagan (Minnesota) School District

PICTURE WINDOW BOOKS
Minneapolis, Minnesota

Editorial Director: Carol Jones
Managing Editor: Catherine Neitge
Creative Director: Keith Griffin
Editor: Christianne Jones
Story Consultant: Terry Flaherty
Designer: Joe Anderson
Page Production: Picture Window Books
The illustrations in this book were created digitally.

Picture Window Books
5115 Excelsior Boulevard
Suite 232
Minneapolis, MN 55416
877-845-8392
www.picturewindowbooks.com

Printed in the United States of America.

Library of Congress Cataloging-in-Publication Data
Loewen, Nancy, 1964-
That costs two shells : the history of money / written by
Nancy Loewen ; illustrated by Brian Jensen.
p. cm. — (Money matters)
Includes bibliographical references and index.
ISBN 1-4048-1159-1 (hardcover)
1. Money—History—Juvenile literature. I. Jensen,
Brian, ill. II. Title. III. Money matters (Minneapolis,
Minn.)

HG221.5.L5342 2006
332.4'9—dc22   2005004066

After supper, Scott opened his backpack. He looked at a flyer about the after-school program at the public library. The program was called That Costs Two Shells: The History of Money.

"Can I go to this?" Scott asked his mom.

"Sure," she said.
"That looks like fun."

AFTER SCHOOL
at the library

The next afternoon, Scott headed to the library. There were shells, stones, metal tools, animal hides, a basket of wheat, some old dried leaves, and a necklace made out of beads. Scott was confused. What was all this stuff?

4

"Don't worry, you came to the right place!" a woman said. "My name is Mrs. Gates, and this is Mr. Willer. We're going to talk to you today about the history of money."

"Believe it or not, all of these objects were once used as money," said Mr. Willer.

Money is something that is used by a community of people as a type of exchange.

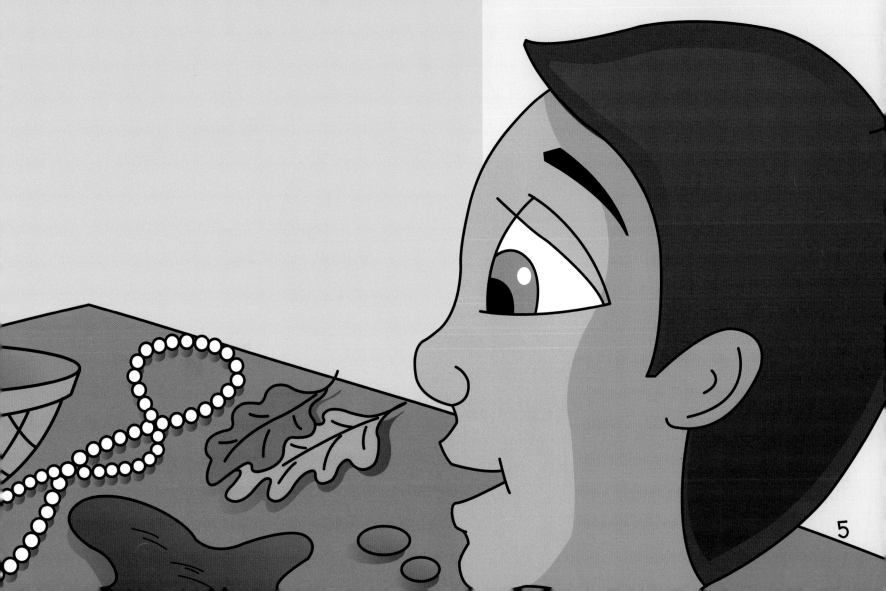

5

"The history of money starts with trading," Mr. Willer said. "Imagine if I traded a pumpkin for an ax from my neighbor. People used to trade food, animal skins, and tools for things they needed. As they became more skillful at growing crops and raising animals, direct trading didn't work so well anymore. Can anyone think why that might be?" he asked.

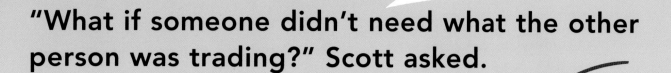

"What if someone didn't need what the other person was trading?" Scott asked.

"Exactly," said Mr. Willer.

In prehistoric times, people didn't need money. They hunted and gathered what they needed to survive.

7

"People soon started to think in a more symbolic way," Mr. Willer explained. "They gave a value to things like animals and food. That way, it didn't matter if someone actually needed a goat. They knew a goat was worth a certain amount. If they didn't want it, they could trade it again for something else."

"So animals and grain were the first kinds of money?" asked Joe.

"That's right," said Mr. Willer. "But even that turned into a problem."

Many historians believe that writing developed out of the need to keep track of trading.

Mrs. Gates held up a basket of small shells.

"These are called cowrie shells," she said.

"The Chinese began using cowries as money around 1,200 B.C. Later, other cultures used cowries as well, including India, Thailand, and Africa. In fact, in the country of Nigeria, cowries were used as late as 1935. That's less than a hundred years ago."

The cowrie shell has been used longer and across a larger area than any other kind of currency.

On the Yap island in the Pacific ocean, native people still use stone discs as money. The larger discs are up to 12 feet (4 meters) across and are too heavy to move.

12

"All sorts of things have been used as money in different cultures and at different periods in history," Mr. Willer said. "Feathers, salt, and beads are just a few examples. Some people even used hunks of metal. What form of money do you think that led to?" Mr. Willer asked.

"Coins!" Scott yelled.

"That's right!" said Mr. Willer.

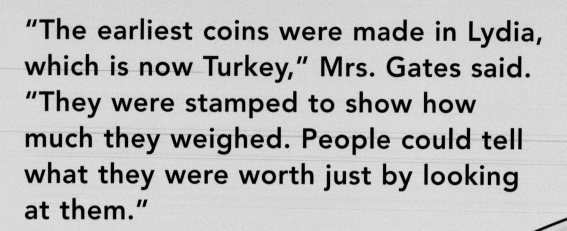

"The earliest coins were made in Lydia, which is now Turkey," Mrs. Gates said. "They were stamped to show how much they weighed. People could tell what they were worth just by looking at them."

She brought out a tray of old coins. "The practice of using coins spread to Greece, Italy, and throughout Europe. The coins were stamped with images of gods, kings, animals, or special designs. In a way, the coins became art, too."

The first coins were made of electrum, a mixture of gold and silver that occurs in nature.

"Ancient coins are very valuable," Mr. Willer added. "These are copies. If you want to see the real thing, a lot of museums have great collections."

"Coins made it easier to manage money," said Mrs. Gates. "But they could still be a burden. Imagine if your parents had to drag a bag of quarters to the grocery store!"

"Along came paper money," said Mr. Willer. "The first paper money was developed in China in the early 10th century. At that time, the coins in China were made of heavy iron. People got tired of carrying them around. So, they left the coins with merchants for handwritten receipts. The receipts said how much money was there. Then, the government took over, printing receipts with fixed values."

"In Europe," added Mrs. Gates, "paper money wasn't widely used until the 1700s."

In 1661, Sweden issued the first official bank notes in Europe. Then came France, in 1720, England, in 1797, and Germany, in 1806.

"Money has gone through many changes," said Mr. Willer. "From cows, to coins, to cash! Money is even changing right now. More and more, people are using money on computer networks. Their paychecks might be deposited directly into their bank accounts. They can pay many of their bills by transferring money electronically. In fact, in the future, people might not need actual money at all."

Within the last ten years, in terms of dollar value, more than 90 percent of all money transactions were made electronically.

"But while the form of money changes, its meaning stays the same," said Mrs. Gates. "Whether it's a basket of grain, a credit card, or a computer, money will always be a symbol of the things people need and want."

After the program, Scott and the other kids gathered around the table. Scott knew these ancient coins weren't real, but it was still kind of neat to imagine.

What's on U.S. Money?

George Washington: First President of the United States

one penny = 1 cent

 Lincoln Memorial

 Abraham Lincoln (16th president)

one nickel = 5 cents

 Monticello (Thomas Jefferson's House)

 Thomas Jefferson (3rd president)

one dime = 10 cents

 A torch with an olive branch on the left and an oak branch on the right

 Franklin D. Roosevelt (32nd president)

one quarter = 25 cents

 Presidential Coat of Arms

 George Washington (1st president)

Great Seal of the United States of America

13-step Pyramid

Glossary

bank notes—paper money; also called bills and cash

currency—the type of money a country uses

deposited—putting money into an account

merchants—people who sell things

mint—where money is made

receipt—a piece of paper printed by the cash register that lists each item that was bought and its price

symbolic—representing, or standing for, something else

transactions—exchanges of money, goods, or services

transferring—moving from one account to another

23

To Learn More

At the Library

Anderson, Jon. *Money: A Rich History*. New York: Grosset and Dunlap, 2003.

Giesecke, Ernestine. *From Seashells to Smart Cards: Money and Currency*. Chicago: Heinemann Library, 2002.

Maestro, Betsy. *The Story of Money*. New York: HarperTrophy, 1995.

On the Web

FactHound offers a safe, fun way to find Web sites related to this book. All of the sites on FactHound have been researched by our staff.
www.facthound.com

1. Visit the FactHound home page.

2. Enter a search word related to this book, or type in this special code: 1404811591

3. Click on the FETCH IT button.

Your trusty FactHound will fetch the best sites for you!

Look for all of the books in the Money Matters series:

- **Cash, Credit Cards, or Checks:** A Book About Payment Methods
- **In the Money:** A Book About Banking
- **Lemons and Lemonade:** A Book About Supply and Demand
- **Let's Trade:** A Book About Bartering
- **Save, Spend, or Donate?** A Book About Managing Money
- **Taxes, Taxes!** Where the Money Goes
- **Ups and Downs:** A Book About the Stock Market
- **That Costs Two Shells:** The History of Money